The subject matter and vocabulary have been selected with expert assistance, and the brief and simple text is printed in large, clear type.

Children's questions are anticipated and facts presented in a logical sequence. Where possible, the books show what happened in the past and what is relevant today.

Special artwork has been commissioned to set a standard rarely seen in books for this reading age and at this price.

Full-colour illustrations are on all 48 pages to give maximum impact and provide the extra enrichment that is the aim of all Ladybird Leaders.

A Ladybird Leader

man
on the sea

Written by James Webster
Illustrated by Gerald Witcomb and Frank Humphris

Publishers: Ladybird Books Ltd . Loughborough
© Ladybird Books Ltd 1974
Printed in England

The first boats

Tree trunks can float.
They were the first boats.

The first canoes were hollow logs.

A few years ago, this raft
sailed across the Pacific Ocean.
It was made of logs tied together.
The first rafts were also
made of logs tied together.

The Kon-tiki

Moving boats by man-power

Once, boats were pushed along.

Some were paddled.
Some were rowed.

Even today, some small boats
are pushed, paddled or rowed.

*A warship of
Ancient Greece*

Boats can use the wind

A boat can be blown along
if it has a sail.
This Viking ship had a sail.
The sail helped the rowers.

When ships had more sails,
they did not need rowers.

Columbus crossed the Atlantic
in a ship like this.

Ships in the Middle Ages

When ships were used for fighting,
'castles' were built at each end.
These protected the soldiers.
The deck at the front of a ship
is still known as the 'forecastle'
or fo'c'sle.

Fighting ships of the 16th century

Openings for cannons were made
in the sides of fighting ships.
The cannons fired solid iron balls.
These ripped holes in enemy ships.

Later, some ships carried as many as a hundred cannons.

A large cannon could sink a ship a thousand yards (914.4 metres) away

Pirates

Some ships were sailed by pirates.
They attacked other ships
and robbed them.

Ships with engines and paddles

Sailing ships were made of wood.
The first iron ships had engines.
The engines were driven by steam,
and turned big paddle wheels.

See what happens

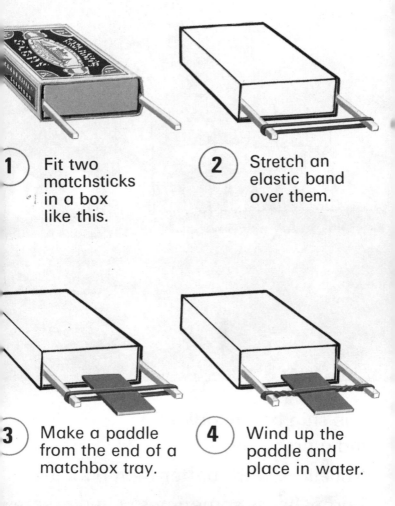

1. Fit two matchsticks in a box like this.

2. Stretch an elastic band over them.

3. Make a paddle from the end of a matchbox tray.

4. Wind up the paddle and place in water.

Ships with engines and propellers

This ship had paddles
and a propeller.

Propellers work better than paddles.

A propeller is sometimes called a 'screw

How a paddle wheel works.

How a screw works.

The last great sailing ships

The last great sailing ships
were the 'clippers' of 100 years ago.
They raced each other home
with cargoes from China and Australia
They carried tea from China
and wool from Australia.

Ports for ships

Liner

Tug

Cargo S

Tug

Tanker

Tug

A port is a place where ships load
and unload.

In big ports you may see liners,
cargo ships, tankers and tugs.

Disaster at sea

This great liner, the Titanic,
hit an iceberg in 1912.
The liner sank very quickly.
Many people were drowned.

A ship that gives warning

There is always danger at sea.
Ships can hit rocks or wrecks.
A lightship warns other ships
of hidden danger.

Boats that save lives

When a ship is in trouble,
a lifeboat goes to her aid.

Lifeboatmen have saved many lives
around the coast of Britain.

Food from the sea

Fish is an important food.
This ship is a trawler.
It pulls a big net, or trawl,
which catches the fish.

The whale hunters

A whaler is a ship that hunts whales.
Too many whales have been killed
for their oil and meat.
The dead whales are pulled in
at the stern (back) of the whaler.

Special boats and ships

A fireboat has water cannon.
It puts out fires on ships.

The front of a ship is called the bows.
An icebreaker has extra strong bows.
It can break very thick ice.
Other ships can then follow it.

Fighting ships of today

These modern frigates
are fast and well armed.
They have skilled crews.

Warships of today
have many electrical aids.

These help their guns to hit targets
even if they are out of sight.

Aircraft carriers

A ship like this is
a floating air base.

Aircraft from it can bomb targets
hundreds of kilometres away.
It carries 'strike' aircraft
and helicopters.

37

Ships that travel under the water

This is a modern submarine.

It can go round the world,
staying under water all the time.
It can fire missiles that travel
thousands of kilometres.

Ships for holidays

People have holidays on modern liner
They swim, sunbathe
and play games
on the deck.

Sailing for sport

There are many kinds of sailing boats.
These large boats are racing.
Today, many people sail for sport.

The world's largest liner

The 'France' is the world's largest lin
She is 1,035 feet (315.5 metres) long
and can travel at 31 knots.

The 'France' carries 2,000 passengers and 1,000 crew.

The hydrofoil

The hydrofoil skims on the water.
It is faster than most boats.

The hovercraft

The hovercraft rides on jets of air.
It can skim over land or water
and travel much faster than a boat.

Ships that can dig

Harbours and rivers fill up with mud.
Dredgers can dig this out.
Their buckets scoop up the mud.
Some dredgers pump up mud.

Ships that carry cars

A ship built to carry cars
is called a car-ferry.

Cars can be driven on or off
at either end.

The old and the new

In 1492, Columbus sailed across
the Atlantic in the Santa Maria.
People thought his ship was big.
The crossing took 5 weeks.

This is how big his ship would look
next to a modern liner.

Now liners cross the Atlantic
in 5 days.

Oil can kill !

This big tanker was wrecked.
Its oil went into the sea.
The oil floated to the shore.

Many fish and sea-birds
were killed.

As tankers get bigger,
this could happen more often.

An early sailing ship

A paddle steamer

A clipper

A modern liner